Memoirs
~ of a ~
Lost Soul

by
Steven James Long

PublishAmerica
Baltimore

© 2004 by Steven James Long.
All rights reserved. No part of this book may be reproduced, stored in a retrieval system or transmitted in any form or by any means without the prior written permission of the publishers, except by a reviewer who may quote brief passages in a review to be printed in a newspaper, magazine or journal.

First printing

ISBN: 1-4137-5685-9
PUBLISHED BY PUBLISHAMERICA, LLLP
www.publishamerica.com
Baltimore

Printed in the United States of America

dedicated to Nicola Marie Foster

A King With No Queen

When the love leaves the heart
And an ache fills the space
The soul slowly saddens
As tears stream the face

Left now once more
To a fate yet unknown
Like a king with no queen
By himself on the throne

The love was so special
Such a bond never known
Now I face up to life
Once again, all alone

Alone

Alone
Empty is the shell
Picked up by the wind
To float into the dreaded mists
Where no one knows your name

Fragile in the grip
Of iron clad abandonment
Ragged and raw
Tattered remnants of love remain

Former porcelain beauty
Shattered into despair
Lay on slabs so cold
As ice now pumps the heart
No longer love
Alone

A Beautiful Flower

A beautiful flower
Now lost in the breeze
All worries and suffering
So peaceful at ease
You touched all around you
With your sparkle and shine
I felt lonely and friendless
But you became mine
There's a void in our lives now
It's barren and bare
Only you seemed to fill it
Now you're no longer there
We loved you so Nicky
But you'll never know
How deep we so cared
Because you had to go
Now we know you're at peace
We're not bitter, nor sour
We will watch you to heaven
A beautiful flower

Love of the Angels

Angels dance on silver clouds
Their voices sweet with tune
As twinkling stars play symphonies
The sun dances with the moon

Cascading lights that catch your eyes
Reflect the deepest love
Then I know I found my kindred soul
As it's written up above

Blank Faces

Blank faces, once a constant sight
Ghost past me into darkened night
Anonymous, No feelings clear
Yet, I dare not shed a tear

Is that you? With whom I'd talk
My partner on life's cautious walk
A face ingrained into my mind
No recognition do I find

I knew you once. I'm sure. I know
Such memories and thoughts now flown
No longer here. Not meant to last
Blank faces ghost into the past

Memories

Do you remember when
I saw you and shook
You took my hand and calmed me
As if poissiden had cast a hand
Over torrent waves
Do you remember when
I cried so hard
And you caught every tear
In your soft, soft heart
Do you remember when
You took my heart
And cradled it
Like an infant child
Do you remember when
You said you marry me
Injecting life into
My Crumbled soul
Do you remember when
You held me while I slept
Walking me towards
The sweetest dreams
I remember
Do you remember?

True Love

Gentle touch
Of trembling hand
Two naked hearts
That understand

That true passion of flesh
Requires a trust
An emotional bond
Beyond the boundaries of lust
As you lay both together
In sensual depth
The world stops around you
As if it's bereft
Of the turn of its axle
And time sets in stone
Two souls become one
No longer alone

Hawk

Hawk, swift in flight to yonder perch
Your grace defines the sky
Such elegance in gliding strokes
Encapsulates the eye

Defy the yearn of gravity
In heavens you do soar
With beauty unsurpassed by none
Withheld since days of yore

Your tranquility, although sublime
Is mirrored with aggression
To stalk your prey and then display
Such predatory possession

kiss

Is it heaven itself?
Two souls intertwined?
An expression of love
That words can't define?

Is it the beat of your heart?
The deepest of trust?
The spirit of passion?
Emotional lust?

Is it the warmest of comforts?
A spiritual bliss.
Is it all of these things?
Or is it just a kiss?

Massacre of Roses

Lighting flash and thunder crack
The sky turns black with fear
Shards of glass do pierce the sky
As malevolent storms draw near

A massacre of roses starts
As flowers crash unto the ground
The rain becomes the flowers blood
And the petals make no sound

A howling of wolves in the wind
Is ominous to all those below
The sky's turned from Jekyll to Hyde
And in its monstrous guise it does grow

The eye of destruction now turning to blue
To the Hyde side the door gently closes
In the aftermath of Zeus's wrath
Lay the massacre of roses

In Dreams

Lost loves sharp pain
Now dulled to an ache
You still live in my dreams
Till the moment I wake

You still laugh whilst I'm sleeping
With your comforting glow
As I lay there, you're with me
Till I rise, then you go

Life's Walk

May we walk through this life
Hand in hand, side by side
Being there for each other
Enjoying the ride

May our paths never stray
Let us walk both together
From moonlight till sunrise
Together, forever

Our bond is so special
It's pure and it's true
And if the walk we shares hard
Then I'll carry you

The Devil's Grasp

No redeeming features will they find
No matter how they probe the mind
Condemned to fate in brimstone heat
Such finalities are now complete

To sign your name on Satan's scroll
Relinquishes your moral soul
Thoughtless actions all despise
Have broke the will and sparked demise

Society has banished thee
It's turned the lock and snapped the key
Outside and in the wilderness
Upon the edge of hells abyss

Walk cautiously with knowing care
Within the grasp of Satan's lair
One fatal slip, one clumsy error
Will plunge you into nightmare terror

To live a life, a life that's whole
Requires a pure, unblemished soul
Yet, this ideal is fantasy
So Lucifer has stolen thee

Patronizing Puppets

Patronizing puppets
On a governmental thread
Dictated to by protocol
As if they're blindly led

Empty words of empathy
A power that's abused
As they line you up like lab rats
Just waiting to be used

They pump you full of poisons
So that they may keep control
They pollute the very essence
Of the body, mind and soul

Reflective Thoughts

Reflective thoughts of years gone by
Of wonders we've achieved
Nostalgic memories of long ago
In the web the past has weaved

When summers were hot and it snowed every Christmas
These thoughts now turning to dust
As the light of life fades, though not yet extinguished
In our children, the future we trust

Wonder of the Sky

Rolling mist on emerald vale
Winters moon so soft and pale
Yonder high a beautiful star
A travelers beacon to be seen from afar

A vibrant guide for wandering heart
To lead to another and nay be apart
To cast down euphoric and radiant love
Held in wonder and awe that star up above

My Best Friend

Sweeping winds of time have passed
Gently blowing through the years
From boy to man you've held my hand
And wiped away the tears

Through ill health and adversity
You've gone the extra length
You're more than a mother to my brothers and me
You are our inner strength

Search the Soul

Take a look at yourself
You may like what you see
Take a look at yourself
There's a reason to be

Take a look at yourself
And try not to hide
Take a look at yourself
Search deep inside

Take a look at yourself
And know you'll survive
Take a look at yourself
And again be alive

Love?

There is no equation
No numerical form
It is both tranquil and calm
Yet a fiery storm

Not yet conquered by science
Neither mapped out like land
We know not where it comes from
And it cannot be planned

You cannot market a product
With such sparkle and fizz
As at the end of the day
Who knows what love is?

Sweet Whispers

Whispers in the wind
That float above the fields of gold
Enchanting distant memories
Not forgotten, yet untold

Beauty lay with graciousness
Beneath floral ode's of love
Their petals reach to touch the soul
Held in blazing sun above

We speak again, just like before
Though I know not where to start
Through silver tears, I hear no sound
As your voice is in my heart

Such a fragile life in hectic times
That was hardly allowed to begin
Now gently floats through golden fields
Sweet whispers in the wind

Catching Lifts on the Clouds

Sleepwalking through life
On a tightrope so thin
Catching lifts on the clouds
Before the rainstorm sets in

Weather the storm
Before the storm weathers you
Steer clear of the grey clouds
Seek the comfort in blue

Take a ride on the rainbow
Let the light be your guide
And you won't be alone
I'll be there by your side

Changing Man

All I ask is a chance to change
A chance for us to be happy again
Deep down inside you know it should be
The best team on earth is you and me
You say it's to late, that we should be apart
But remember the good times, look deep in your heart
I'm changing my ways, rebuilding my life
Only one thing is missing, that's you as my wife
I know you are doubting and do not think that it's true
All I ask is a chance and I'll prove it to you

Choices

If only
You weren't such a good friend
If only
Our hearts weren't on the mend
If only
We'd taken a separate path
If only
It wasn't wrong to cuddle and laugh
If only
'Twas a thing that can never be
If only
It could have been that's with me

Cruel World

Innocence lost and reality clear
I see the world from a different view
Where love is a myth and people are cruel
And nothing they say is quite true

We live in a time when people believe
The world is a wonderful place
Yet they fail to acknowledge the wars and the famine
And discrimination against gender and race

Dad

The look in the eyes
Plays a ballad so loud
Conveying warmth and respect
From a father who's proud

The emotionless demeanor
That you used to declare
Now crumbles away
As the eyes show, you care

I felt so neglected
And for years I was sad
But you've shown your true colours
And I love you so, Dad

Daydream Escape

As the thoughts gently wander
On a marmalade breeze
The fairies will guide you
Making sure you're at ease

To the mystical castle
In the purple mist sky
Where you'll sing with the angels
And learn how to fly

Empty Reflections

I look in the mirror
Knowing not what I'll see
No familiar face
Is smiling at me

Blank reflections
Now bore a hole
No smiling face
No joyful soul

Instead, there's a stranger
With a look of despair
Unable to love
Unable to care

Fading Mists

Fading, slowly fading
Into the grey mists of time past
Falling, gently falling
To the withered end at last

Pouted emotional current
Ebbed and free from spark
Life's light slowly walking
On route in to the dark

New life's birth is imminent
This, itself foreboding
For where there is life there is death
Fading, slowly fading

Farewell Nicky

Religious whispers soothe the heart
But cannot dry the tears
Cherish the life that was lived on this earth
That was so tragically cut short in years

The sun shone so brightly and the breeze was so sweet
Not a cloud to be seen up above
The setting was beautiful, just as you were
As we said goodbye to the one that we love

Flawed Heart

Put back to the prison
From which I'd escaped once before
My heart loving, yet fragile
Proved my ultimate flaw

Condemned once again
Unaware of my crime
Only one question remains
Will you visit this time?

Fragile Heart

Please do not play with my heart
As it is not a toy
You could so easily break it
As well as bring joy

My heart's fragile enough
Through worry and strife
The only thing that can fix it
Is you in my life

God's Children

He is all around us
Yet so far away
He seemed so absent
On that fateful day

I reached out towards him
Like never before
But received no response
Perhaps I was flawed

We are all his children
Yet none of us know
When he'll come to collect us
When it's our time to go

Golden Beauty

Pure sunshine gold
Draped on porcelain brow
You fade into shadows
As my thoughts but allow

A brief dreamlike appearance
Of a beauty so pure
When you're here I'm a rich man
When you're gone, oh so poor

Greed

Cosmetic surgeons
Increasing their wealth
Who won't take a pay cut
For the everyman's health

Corrupted and selfish
For personal gain
Heartless black souls
Uncaring and vain

There was once faith in humanity
During wars and through hardship
Now it saddens the soul
That it's money we worship

Heaven's Star

The brightest star I ever did know
The warmest embrace
And radiant glow
I know that I'll miss you

I know that I'll cry
But you'll always be with me
My bright star in the sky

Inspiration

O' wondering thought
That wanders the mind
O' wondering thought
Be you gentle and kind

O' wondering thought
So frequent and sure
O' wondering thought
Be you simple and pure

O' wondering thought
That pulses the heart
O' wondering thought
You've been there from the start

O' wondering thought
Inspirationally giving
O' wondering thought
You're my engine for living

Life's Flow

Like a shrouded black blanket
Draped over your shoulders
Restricting your movement
And weighted like boulders

Like swimming up stream
Driven back by the flow
Like an uncharted map
With nowhere to go

Even the strongest of minds
Find it hard to deny
The purpose of living
When we're waiting to die

Loss of My Angel

A beautiful angel
A heart made of gold
The love of my life
Now bitter and cold

But no one can blame you
Because nobody knew
The pain and the suffering
That I put you through

And now it is my turn
To suffer my pain
To know I will never
Be with you again

Warneford Whispers

Shadows creep along the grass
As the sunlight fades away
The moon arises from its sleep
And the stars come out to play

A mottled blend of blue and black
Paints the canvas way up high
And silver pools of tranquil calm
Reflect the splendor of night sky

As the world gently sleeps, at peace in its dreams
And serenity reigns like a king
I cherish the magic before dawn breaks the spell
And think life's such a wonderful thing

Neptune's Wrath

As we try, yet we struggle
Against the waves
With no hope, but futility
Like shackled down slaves

And inmates we are
Of the ocean we're in
Where some of us drown
Yet, some of us swim

Yet, those left afloat
In a sanctuary of bliss
Should cherish the ocean
For below's the abyss

Rage

The inferno is blazing
A fiery rage
The untamed demon
Set free from his cage

Destruction and terror
Lay wake in his trail
He has no emotion
And preys on the frail

His burning black coals
Scorch through to the heart
As he takes all the love
Then tears it apart

There is no redemption
For the beasts lost his soul
And where once was his heart
There's a smoldering hole

Summer Days

Mother Nature took me by the hand
And led me through the trees
To gaze upon the pastoral land
Such beauty brought me to my knees

Sunlight broke the wispy shade
And its haze enveloped me so
I lay there as the fairies played
With no better place to go

I was lost in the daydream
Of a sweet summers day
Watching sparkles on the water gleam
Letting thoughts just skip away

The Lonely Bed

Alone at night in a bed made for two
Left with thoughts that dance through the mind
As you stare at the pillow that's empty beside you
Knowing you've lost something so hard to find

As the days turn to weeks and the weeks turn to months
The pain slowly ebbs to a still
The journey through life continues apace
With a space left beside you to fill

The Reaper's Plea

To escape in a vessel
In a warm sea of red
Like sleeping forever
In the comfiest bed

So peaceful and still
No concept of time
No worries, no heartache
Where everything's fine

How I so long to be there
Away from my woe
Yet there are so many reasons
Not letting me go

Valentine

Valentine o' valentine
If I send you flowers will be mine
If roses their fair scent would be
Would you give your heart alone to me?

Or chocolates o' so sugar sweet
May sweep you off your very feet
A verse perhaps, an ode to you
To show you that my heart is true

O' valentine your beauty charms
I long to have you In my arms
To hold you close in sensual bliss
The gift that I give you is true loves kiss

War Child

On a cold Christmas morning
Lay a child in their bed
There's no joyful emotion
Just a doom laden dread

No fireplace stockings
No presents to give
The best gift they obtain
Is being able to live

As the powers that be
Ignore mans free will
The minority dictate
That the masses should kill

No more family to love
No more life to adore
The only present this year
Is the effect of a war

Yesterday's Life

A trembling fear
Strikes a crippling blow
There is no place to hide
There is no place to go

This place seems so foreign
When once it was home
I visit old haunts
Yet I still feel alone

My world seems so different
How long was I gone?
The faces have changed
And my past has moved on

My home now seems smaller
My friends are now strange
My life's disappeared
Swept up in the change

Warmth of My Fire

With all my heart
I'll love you forever
Through good times and bad
We'll face them together

You're the rose in my garden
The warmth of my fire
The sweet breeze of the sea
You're all I desire

May you pulse through my veins
In trouble and strife
As together, we're one
Because you are my life

This Verse of Mine

What is a poem?
An ode to one's self?
Or just something that's written
Then placed on a shelf

To me it's emotion
Your feelings inside
A way of expressing
What you normally hide

Sunsets

Stood upon the brink
Of golden sky and sand
The crystal ocean bathes the sun
As it comes to meet the land

The wispy trees that stand above
The carpets blonde as hay
Rustle their leaves and bid farewell
To the radiance of day

As the sun slowly sets into comfortable sleep
The moon takes over the shift
To be here together to witness such beauty
Is a truly magical gift

Printed in the United Kingdom
by Lightning Source UK Ltd.
106534UKS00001B/177